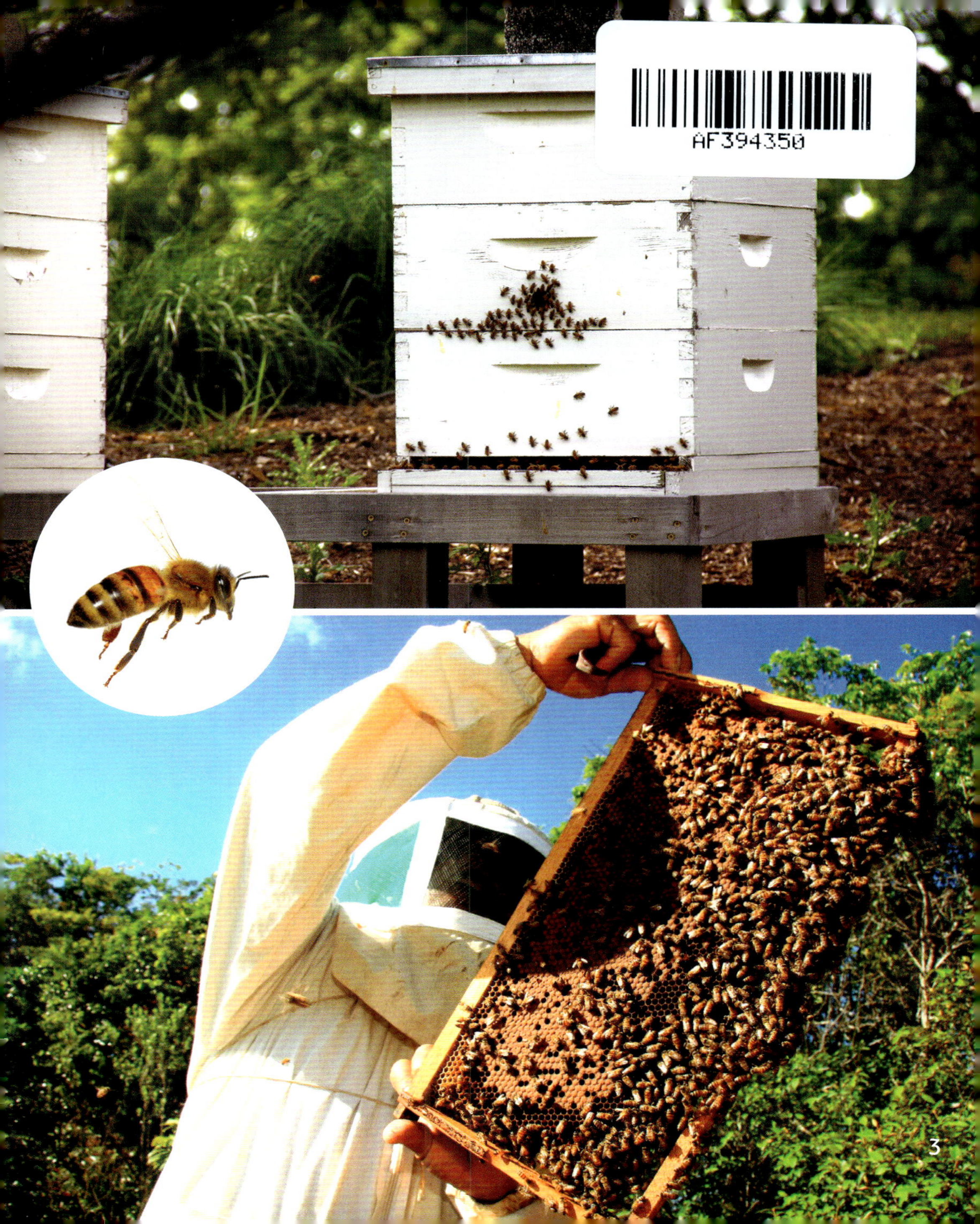
AF394350

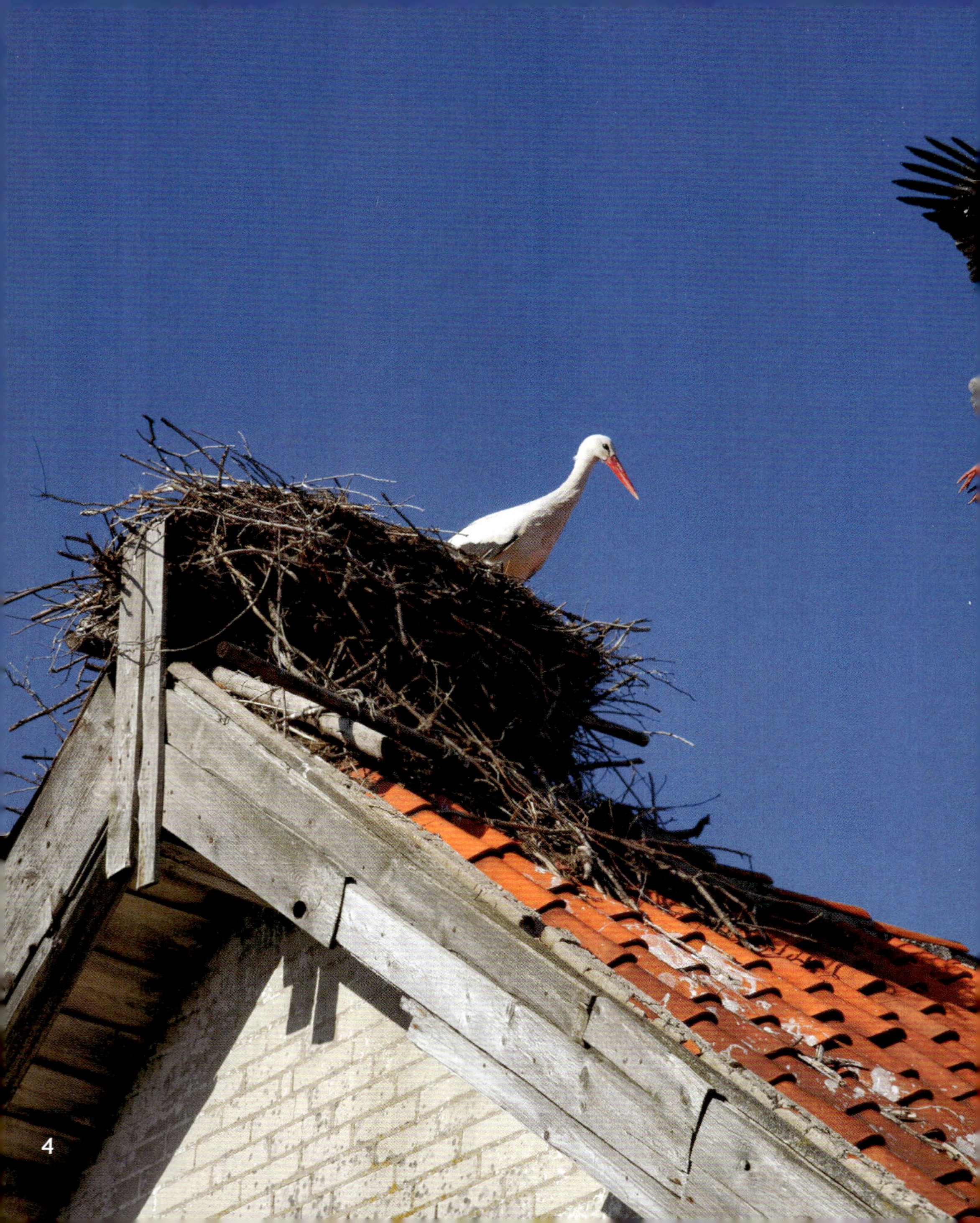

Animal Homes

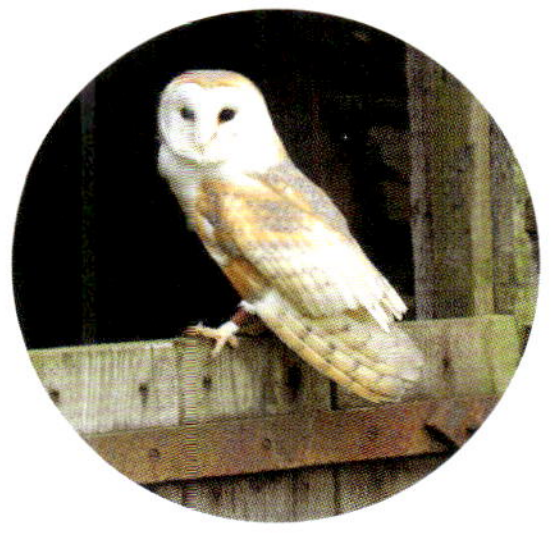

Written by
Stephen Rickard

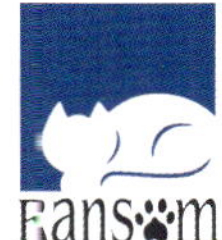

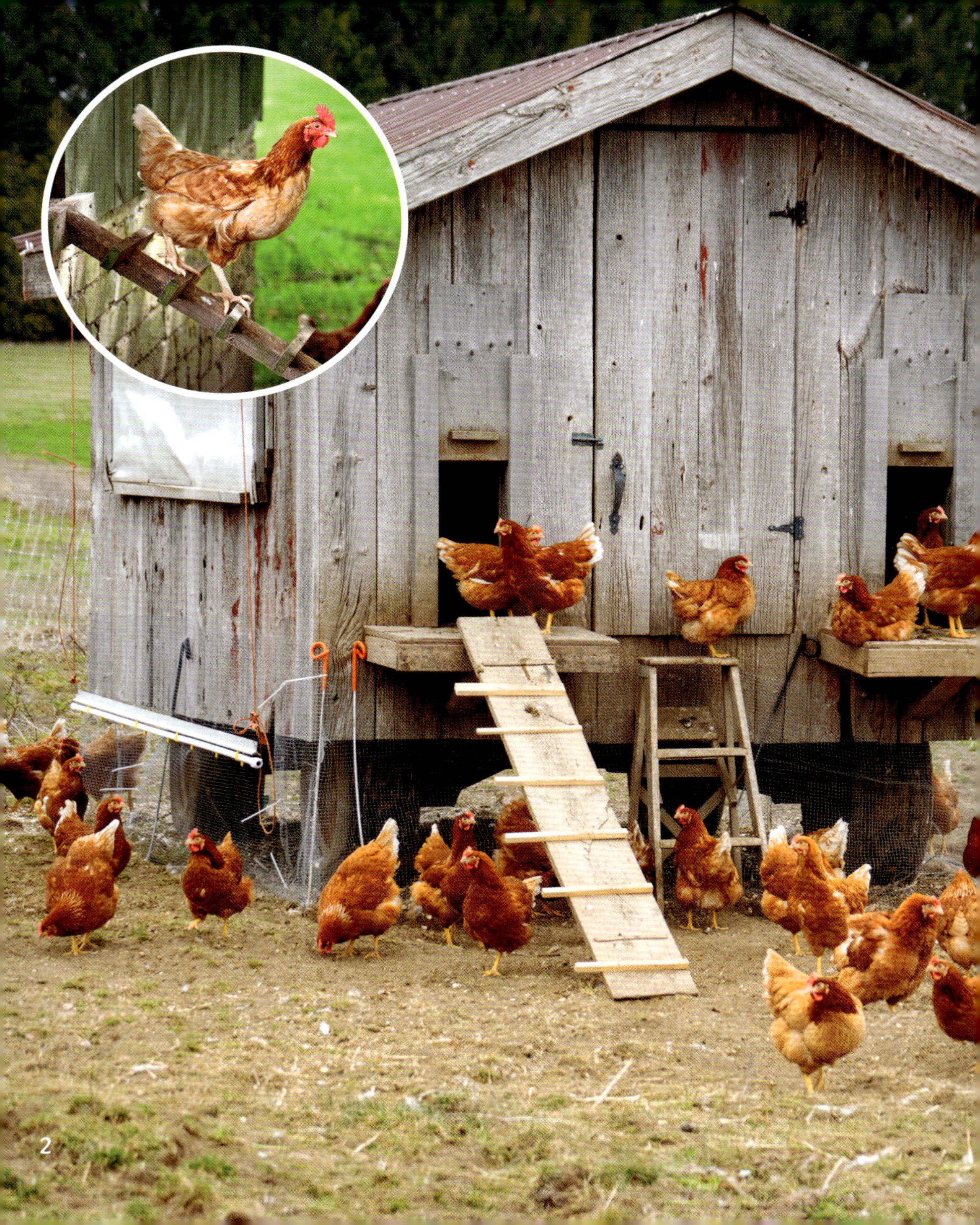

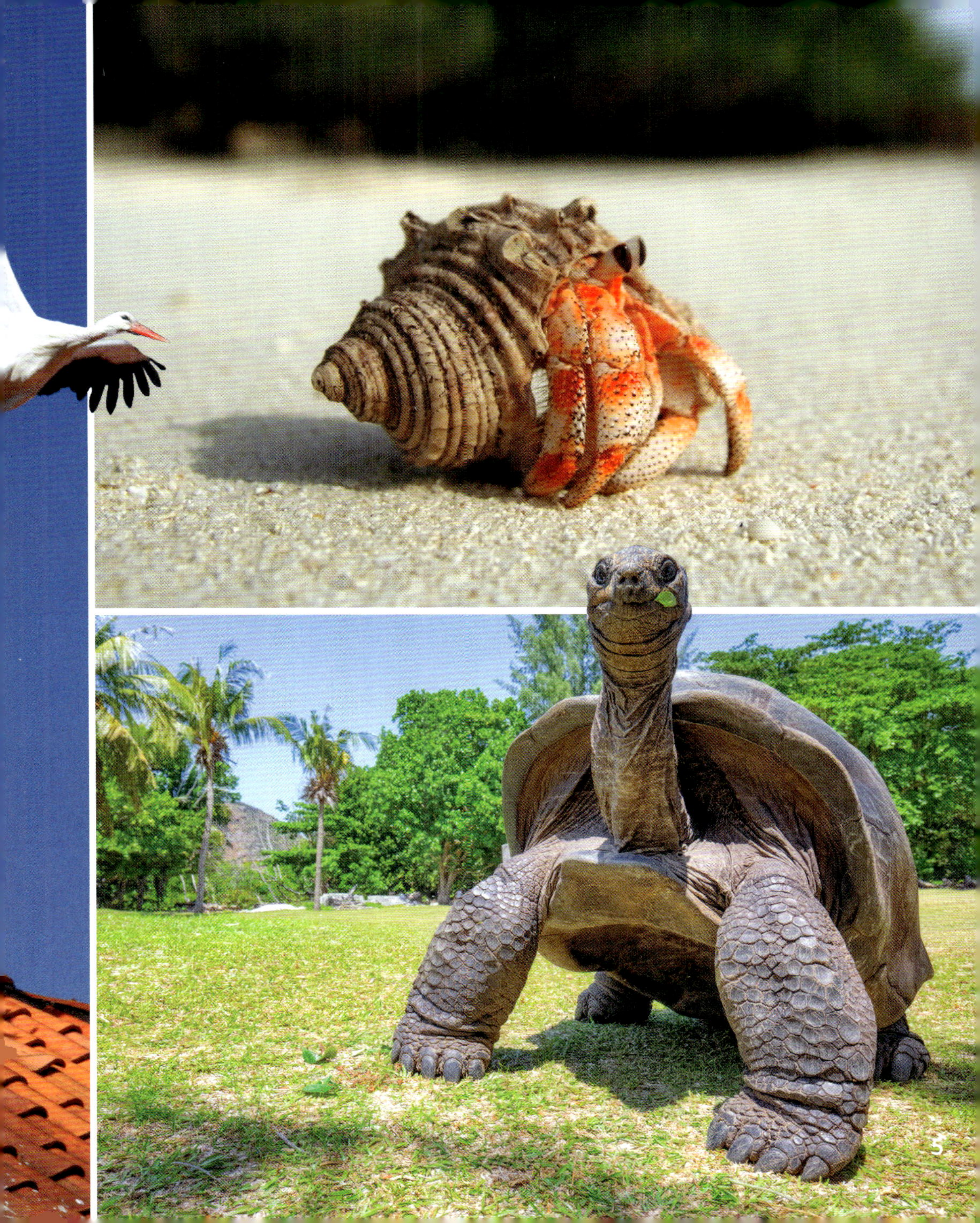

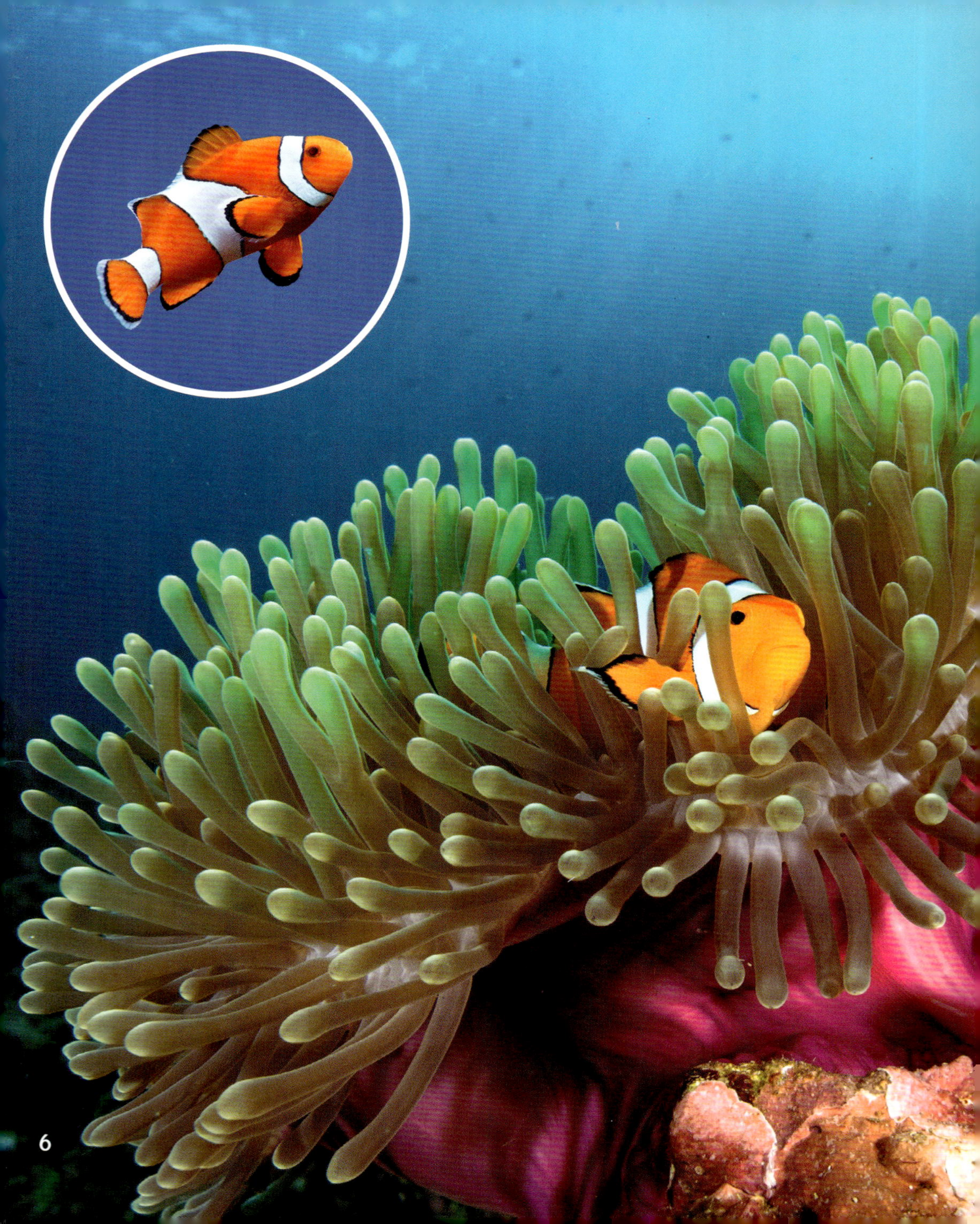

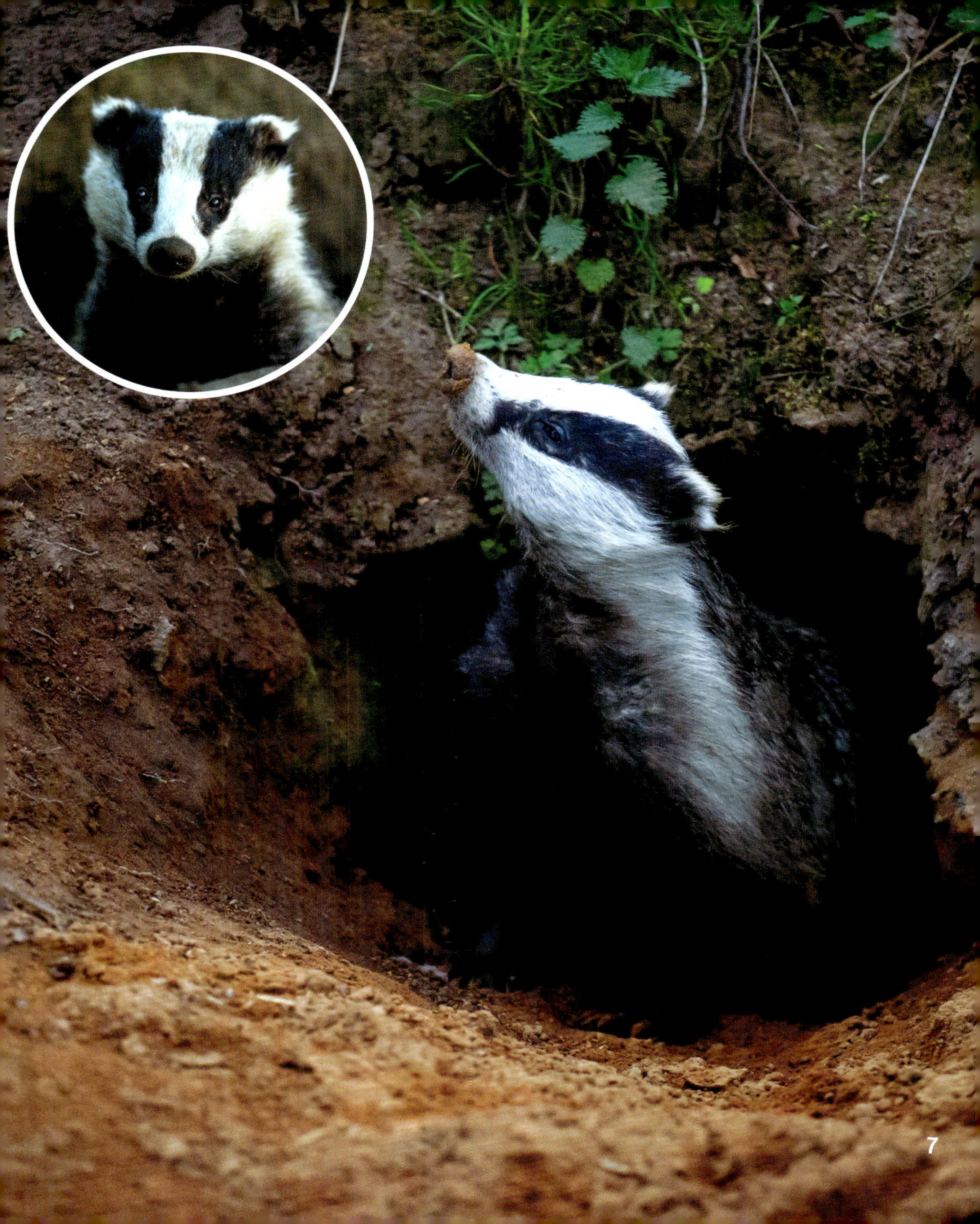

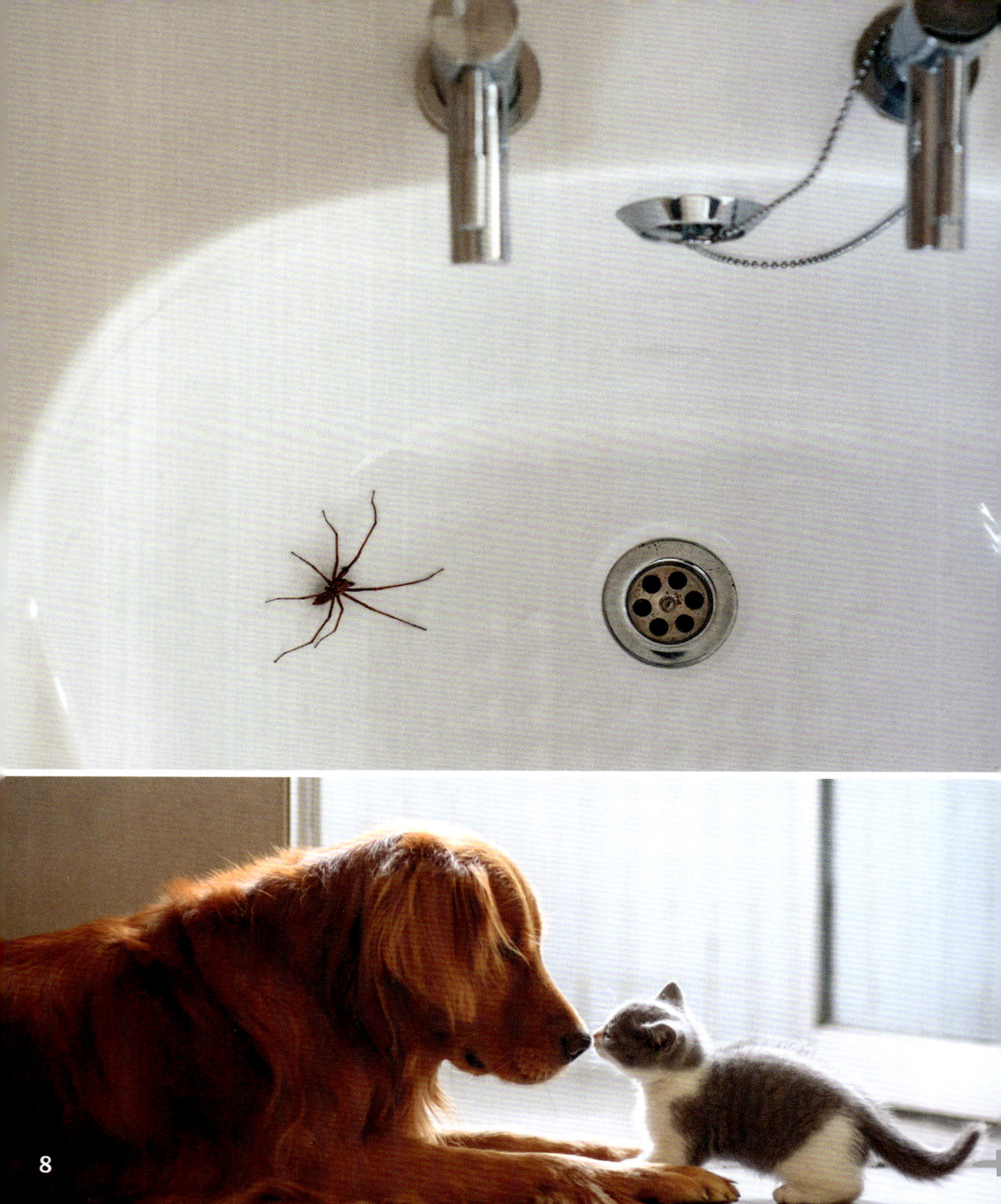